Veteran
Season

DISCIPLING NEW CHRISTIANS

With the Spiritual T.E.A.M.

by John Hendee

STANDARD PUBLISHING
Cincinnati, Ohio

3246

Contents

SPIRITUAL T.E.A.M.

COVENANT

Knowing what is expected of a T.E.A.M. member, I promise, to the best of by ability, to fulfill the requirements of being on a Spiritual T.E.A.M.

I will be open to growing, caring, maturing, and obeying God's will in my life. I will seek to support those on my T.E.A.M.

T.E.A.M. Members   Date

_______________________________________   _______________

_______________________________________   _______________

_______________________________________   _______________

Coach

_______________________________________   _______________

WHO SAID IT WOULD BE EASY?

Marathon runners seem to agree that the pain in a twenty-six-mile run can become excruciating at points. Some of them also say that there are certain times in the race that are predictable drop-out times. If you get past them and don't quit, then you are home free. One can apparently experience a euphoric state when the body shrugs off pain and freely glides along almost mechanically. To run the marathon takes desire, training, and willingness to hang in there when it hurts!

The same can be said of the Christian life and service. To run the race for Christ one must also have desire, training, and a willingness to hang in there when it hurts. Jesus never said it would be easy.

Paul had the spiritual endurance of a distance runner. He was often hurt, but he never gave up. He kept going even when it was rough. Read the following passages, and list some of the kinds of difficulties he had:

2 Corinthians 1:7______________________________

2 Corinthians 1:8______________________________

2 Corinthians 2:1______________________________

2 Corinthians 2:2______________________________

2 Corinthians 2:4______________________________

2 Corinthians 11:24-29__________________________

2 Corinthians 12:21____________________________

1 Thessalonians 2:9____________________________

2 Timothy 4:10________________________________

2 Timothy 4:14________________________________

2 Timothy 4:16________________________________

A poll showed that in a recent professional football season, the player/injury ratio was 1/1. Some had more than one injury, which made up for the ones who had none. I suppose if we took a year's survey among Christians and found what the servant/injury or "hurt ratio" was, it would be at least 1/1. Do you ever get scraped, rejected, or hurt in your ministry for Christ? Do you ever grieve, hurt, or have sleepless moments in behalf of others? If not, you are probably watching the game from the bleachers. It's hard to get hurt from there. It's hard not to get hurt when you're on the field.

In 2 Timothy 2:3-6, Paul said, "Endure hardship with us like a good soldier of Christ Jesus. . . . if anyone competes as an athlete, he does not receive the victor's crown unless he competes according to the rules. The hardworking farmer should be the first to receive a share of the crops." All three of these groups are willing to sweat, risk danger, and sacrifice now for the anticipated victory in war, winning of the game, or harvesting of the crop. What should you do when you are hurting? Tell God. He'll help; He won't abandon you. You'll learn more things to do in the passages this week.

Strategy Ideas

Personal Planning

In the first column, list any of your recent or current trials, stresses, problems, temptations, or struggles e.g. trouble with job/business, kids, marriage, friend, health, your failures, others' failures, loneliness, or some other). Then, in column 2, be frank about your own responsibility or fault in making the situation a problem. Finally, use column 3 to plan a means of improving the situation.

Problem
What did you do, or are you doing, to add to the problem?

What will you do to help the situation?

T R A I N

"All Scripture is God-breathed and is useful for teaching, rebuking, correcting and training in righteousness, so that the man of God may be thoroughly equipped for every good work."

—2 Timothy 3:16

Daily Training Verses

1. John 16:33
2. John 14:1-4, 27
3. John 16:20-23
4. 2 Corinthians 1:3-7, 10, 11
5. 1 John 5:3-5
6. Galatians 6:7-10

T	R	A	I	N
T—TEACH. What does this passage teach me?	R—REBUKE. Does the passage correct me in any way? Am I satisfied with the extent to which I am applying it?	A—APPLY. If I applied this passage to my life, would I start or stop anything? What? Visualize it.	I—INITIATE. If I can start or stop something, when will I do it? Today? How? With whom?	N—NEEDS. I need to pray. (Follow the ACTS pattern: Adore, Confess, Thank, Supplicate.)

WHAT'S A SUCCESSFUL PLAYER LOOK LIKE?

Not too many set out intentionally seeking to be failures. Not very many who set out intending to be successes are. Part of the difficulty is that many of us have no idea what success really is. Many end up achieving what they had been led to believe was success, only to find out that it can be very empty.

God and the average man have been known to have a slightly different idea and perspective as to what success is.

According to the magazine ads, the TV commercials, the radio spots, and the visible thrust of the American culture, success is any or all of the following: social status, good looks, to be sexy or macho, brains, to wear the right clothes, to have the right friends, to have lots of friends, to have good health, to have a good sense of humor, to be rich (big home, new car, and the like), to hold high positions (to have power), to hold a good job, to have control over people, to eat the best food, and/or to be able to travel extensively.

God's view of success is a little bit different. Most of the above only allow one to accumulate checks on their mental chart for having compiled external achievements by hard work, luck, or pressure. To the one who accumulates these, disaster comes in their loss, and misery is the byword for one who seeks but never finds them. But thanks be to the Lord! Life, its enjoyment, its fulfillment, and its richness, are not dependent on all those. They may add a different dimension to life in some way, but they are not the essence of life.

According to the Scriptures, including Jesus' own life and teachings, success is developing and retaining the following in one's life: contentment in any situation, inner joy, leading a pure life, loving a neighbor as oneself, putting oneself in someone else's place, being persecuted for doing right, being sorry for sin, striving for peace, having right relationships, and self-control. (See Matthew 5:3-10.)

According to the world's view of success, Jesus was a failure: social status (He died as a criminal); looks ("He had no beauty or majesty to attract us to him"—Isaiah 53:2); sexy/macho (He gave up marriage and sex for a mission); brains (didn't flaunt brains, but was very wise); clothes (had few); the right and many friends (His friends all abandoned Him); sense of humor (a man of sorrows"—Isaiah 53:3); rich (wasn't); high position (King without a people); good job (unemployed rabbi). Jesus was no failure. He was the ultimate in success. He came to do the will of His Father, and He did it perfectly. That brought sorrow and suffering to Him, yet it resulted in perfection and joy and eternal life for all who accept His grace.

Whose standard of success are you going to spend your life seeking? The better you know Jesus, the better understanding and model of success you will have.

Strategy Ideas

God is not opposed to a person's looking nice, being intelligent, dressing neatly, having friends, being healthy, or the like. The issue is, are these the end purpose of life, or are they things we are to use to help us as we seek to fulfill God's will of winning the world? (See 1 Corinthians 7:30, 31; Philippians 3:17-21; 4:11.)

Do you spend more time seeking the items in column A or B in your life? Which would your family members think is more important to you by what they see you do?

A	B
social status; good looks	contentment in any situation
to be sexy/macho; brains	inner joy
to wear the right clothes	leading a pure life
to have lots of friends	loving a neighbor as oneself
to have the right friends	putting oneself in someone else's place
good health; good sense of humor	being persecuted for doing right
to be rich; to hold high positions	being sorry for sin
to hold a good job	striving for peace
to have control over people	having right relationships
to eat the best food; to travel	self-control

Personal Planning

T R A I N

"All Scripture is God-breathed and is useful for teaching, rebuking, correcting and training in righteousness, so that the man of God may be thoroughly equipped for every good work."

—2 Timothy 3:16

Daily Training Verses

1. Matthew 6:25-34
2. Matthew 13:44-46
3. Luke 12:13-21
4. Luke 18:18-30
5. Luke 16:19-31
6. Matthew 25:31-46

T—TEACH. What does this passage teach me?	R—REBUKE. Does the passage correct me in any way? Am I satisfied with the extent to which I am applying it?	A—APPLY. If I applied this passage to my life, would I start or stop anything? What? Visualize it.	I—INITIATE. If I can start or stop something, when will I do it? Today? How? With whom?	N—NEEDS. I need to pray. (Follow the ACTS pattern: Adore, Confess, Thank, Supplicate.)
T	**R**	**A**	**I**	**N**

LOVING THE UNLIKABLE TEAM MEMBERS

Along with the many outstanding individuals, you may encounter some pretty dislikable people in the church. (Of course, that would never be us. Who could not like us?) Back to the other guy. Just for a minute, think about a few of the possible unlikable traits in the lives of other Christians:

self-righteousness	disagreeableness	unfriendliness
immaturity	negative attitude	cruelty
wealth	carelessness	gossip
poverty	messy habits	dishonest
pride	laziness	hypocrisy
impatience	procrastination	funny looks
habitual tardiness	lack of reliability	funny voice/
bad breath	critical spirit	accent
poor fashion taste	talkative nature	funny
griping	quiet nature	mannerisms

And so it goes. You may even know some character who seems to be a well-balanced composite of all these!

Now consider the fact that Jesus commanded us to love them! YIKES! How on earth can you possibly love anyone so unlikable? It helps to understand what love is. It is not a feeling or an emotion. Jesus never commanded us to have an emotion, but He did command our actions and attitudes. It's not a question of the others' being lovable, but whether we are loving!

Love is doing what is best for the other, regardless of how you feel about them. That is the only way you can love your enemy. You may not have good feelings for them, but you can treat them in such a way to help them grow toward Christ. Jesus held our love for our fellow Christians (and for all men) as a very high priority.

John said, "This is the message you heard from the beginning: We should love one another" (1 John 3:11). Paul worked with the Thessalonians and gave of himself to them in love. "We loved you so much that we were delighted to share with you not only the gospel of God but our lives as well, because you had become so dear to us" (1 Thessalonians 2:8). They had learned from Paul's example. He said of them, "Now about brotherly love, we do not need to write to you, for you yourselves have been taught by God to love each other. And in fact, you do love all the brothers throughout Macedonia. Yet we urge you, brothers, to do so more and more" (1 Thessalonians 4:9, 10). They couldn't love too much.

If another Christian seems very obnoxious, revolting, annoying, critical, or irritating to you, remember he is a great opportunity for you to demonstrate your love and maturity in Christ!

Strategy Ideas

List some people you don't like: they've irritated you, rejected you or hurt you, in some way.	What did they do, or what are they like, that you don't like?	How did or do you react to them?	Is your reaction to and treatment of them Christlike? If no, how could you make it so?
1.			
2.			
3.			
4.			
5.			

List some people from whom you are now alienated.	In your view, what caused the alienation?	Was and is your reaction to them Christlike?	What can you do to reconcile the relationship?
1.			
2.			
3.			
4.			
5.			

Personal Planning

T R A I N

"All Scripture is God-breathed and is useful for teaching, rebuking, correcting and training in righteousness, so that the man of God may be thoroughly equipped for every good work."

—2 Timothy 3:16

Daily Training Verses

1. John 15:9-14
2. 1 Peter 3:8-12
3. 1 Thessalonians 5:11-15
4. Philippians 2:1-4
5. Colossians 3:12-14
6. 1 John 3:14-18

T	R	A	I	N
T—TEACH. What does this passage teach me?	R—REBUKE. Does the passage correct me in any way? Am I satisfied with the extent to which I am applying it?	A—APPLY. If I applied this passage to my life, would I start or stop anything? What? Visualize it.	I—INITIATE. If I can start or stop something, when will I do it? Today? How? With whom?	N—NEEDS. I need to pray. (Follow the ACTS pattern: Adore, Confess, Thank, Supplicate.)

MAKING THE OTHER PLAYERS LOOK GOOD

To the average person, the word *submission* immediately prompts a mental image of a wife running around, frantically trying to fulfill her husband's every wish and whim. It's a distasteful image, and thus a distasteful word. This is unfortunate. Submission is a part of every Christian's life (not just wives'), but it is much different from the picture just described. It is certainly not blind obedience.

In a sense, *submission* means the same as *love*, *serve*, or *obey*. The common ground in all these words is a willingness to advance the best interest of another, even at the expense of one's own interests. When I love someone, I do what is best for him—even if I have to sacrifice some of my own time, money, or effort. Jesus said, "Love each other as I have loved you" (John 15:12).

Submission to another means helping that person become like Christ by treating him as Christ would. It means to encourage, set an example, or support. (See Galatians 6:2.)

In that sense, even leaders submit to the persons who follow them. Real authority has a submissive nature. (See 1 Thessalonians 2:7-12.) Having one in submission to you doesn't mean you give arbitrary commands; it means you submit your own interests to the good of the whole—to the purpose for which you were called to lead. First Peter 5:1-5 and Matthew 20:24-27 point out the submissive (servant) nature of real leadership.

A disciple must not put his own interests before the best interests of another. For a disciple, *submission* means he will not press his own will, but will subject his will to the interests of another disciple and of the church as a whole, Christ's body. In other words, he submits his will to Christ.

The best interest of every disciple is to be like Christ. Thus, I will do nothing to detract or interfere with another's growth. I'll do what I can to help others grow into Christlikeness.

Christians are commanded to submit to one another—Ephesians 5:21; Philippians 2:4. Wives are to submit to their husbands—Ephesians 5:22; 1 Peter 3:1. Men are to submit to older men—1 Timothy 5:1; 1 Peter 5:5. Christians are to submit to authorities, such as government—1 Peter 2:13; Romans 13:1. Christians are to submit to church leaders—Hebrews 13:7.

In the New Covenant, one is called to a way of life that requires that we submit to all our fellow disciples—to do all we can to help them become more Christlike. There is no room for selfish ambition in the church. We all cooperate, support, and encourage one another to make everyone a success.

Strategy Ideas

Notice the mutual submission in the following pairs of statements.

1. *The church* is to submit itself to *Christ*, to accomplish His will on earth (Ephesians 1:22, 23).

   Christ submitted himself to the *church*, to make it a success (Ephesians 5:25).

2. *Husbands* are to submit to their *wives*, making them a success in Christ's eyes (Ephesians 5:21-25).

   Wives are to submit to their *husbands*, making them a success in Christ's eyes (Ephesians 5:21-25).

3. *Children* are to submit to their *parents*, making them a success in Christ's eyes (Ephesians 6:1ff).

   Parents are to submit to their *children*, making them a success in Christ's eyes (Ephesians 6:4).

4. *Slaves* are to submit to their *leaders*, making them a success in Christ's eyes (Ephesians 6:5-8).

   Masters are to submit to their *slaves*, making them a success in Christ's eyes (Ephesians 6:9).

5. *Church leaders* (elders) are to submit to their *members*, making them a success in Christ's eyes (Hebrews 13:17).

   Church members are to submit to their *leaders*, making them a success in Christ's eyes (Hebrews 13:7).

6. *Citizens* are to submit to their *governors*, making them a success in Christ's eyes (Romans 13:1, 5).
Governors are to submit to their *citizens*, making them a success in Christ's eyes (Romans 13:3, 4).

Now complete the following chart to determine ways you can be submissive in a Scriptural way. Then read "Being an Actor Instead of a Reactor," which follows.

Person	What are you doing to help them become like Christ, to advance their best interests, or to help them to be successful in God's eyes?	What could you do to demonstrate love/submission?
Mate		
Child/Children		
Parents		
Church Leaders		
Government Leaders		
Neighbors		
Boss		
Employees		
Poor/Rich		

I walked with my friend, a Quaker, to the newsstand the other night, and he bought a paper, thanking the newsman politely. The newsman didn't even acknowledge it.

"A sullen fellow, isn't he," I commented.

"Oh, he's that way every night," shrugged my friend.

"Then why do you continue being so polite to him?" I asked.

"Why not?" inquired my friend. "Why should I let *him* decide how I'm going to act?"

As I thought about this little incident later, it occurred to me that the operating word was "act." My friend "acts" toward people; most of us react toward them.

He has a sense of inner balance lacking in most of us frail and uncertain creatures; he knows who he is, what he stands for, and how he should behave. No boor is going to disturb the equilibrium of his nature; he simply refuses to return incivility with incivility, because then he would no longer be in command of his own conduct, but a mere responder to others.

When we are enjoined in the Bible to return good for evil, we look upon this as a moral injuction, which it is; but it is also a psychological prescription for our emotional health.

Nobody is unhappier than the perpetual reactor. His center of emotional gravity is not rooted within himself, where it belongs, but in the world outside him. His spiritual temperature is always being raised or lowered by the social climate around him, and he is a mere creature at the mercy of these elements.

Praise gives him a feeling of euphoria, which is false, because it does not last and it does not come from self-approval. Criticism depresses him more than it should, because it confirms his own secretly shaky opinion of himself. Snubs hurt him, and the merest suspicion of unpopularity in any quarter rouses him to bitterness, aggressiveness or complaint.

Only a saint, of course, *never* reacts. But a serenity of spirit cannot be achieved until we become the masters of our own actions and attitudes, and not merely the passive reactors to other persons' feelings. To let another determine whether we shall be rude or gracious, elated or depressed, is to relinquish control over our own personalities, which is ultimately all we possess. The only true possession is self-possession.

My friend is a model of balanced conduct, and few of us can hope to attain his kind of surefootedness. But we can at least adjust our weight to lean less heavily upon the world's giddy gyrations.

by Sidney Harris, syndicated column.

Personal Planning

T R A I N

"All Scripture is God-breathed and is useful for teaching, rebuking, correcting and training in righteousness, so that the man of God may be thoroughly equipped for every good work."

—2 Timothy 3:16

Daily Training Verses

1. Ephesians 5:21
2. 1 Peter 5:1-5
3. Matthew 20:24-28
4. 1 Timothy 5:1, 2
5. 1 Peter 2:13, 17; 3:7; 4:8
6. Philippians 2:4; 1 Corinthians 16:16

T—TEACH. What does this passage teach me?	R—REBUKE. Does the passage correct me in any way? Am I satisfied with the extent to which I am applying it?	A—APPLY. If I applied this passage to my life, would I start or stop anything? What? Visualize it.	I—INITIATE. If I can start or stop something, when will I do it? Today? How? With whom?	N—NEEDS. I need to pray. (Follow the ACTS pattern: Adore, Confess, Thank, Supplicate.)

T	R	A	I	N

THE CRITIC IN THE BLEACHERS AND ON THE BENCH

Have you ever had the experience of going to an organized sports game and watching the fans in the bleachers and the players on the bench? Every team has fans who do nothing but sit in the bleachers criticizing every move of the coach and every action of the players. They seem assured that they know how to play the game better, and they are quite vocal about making it known. (Notice, though, that they never play the game; they just criticize. Apparently, they think that buying their tickets earns them the right.) You can also find players on sports teams who are continually critical of the coach and the other players.

Well, sorry to disappoint you, but even if you failed to notice, there are critics in the church. They are like self-appointed theater critics who major in, and seem to delight in, tearing down others. They remind us of buzzards searching for dead flesh. When they spot the decaying remains of some hapless creature, they get their friends together to feast on the foulness. "Why couldn't they be more like honeybees?" we wonder. They are very particular about finding only the sweetest and best nectar as they fly among the beautiful flowering plants.

There are both bees and buzzards in the church, and you can be either one. It just depends on what you look for. Do you look for foulness or sweetness? The buzzard and the bee both find what they look for.

There are many bees in the church, a number of good examples of positive team members who are encouraging and uplifting. One man who is like a bee is Dale Hudson. Dale is a counselor at Mesa High School, Mesa, Arizona, and an elder at Central Christian Church in Mesa. Dale has the rare an genuine habit of greeting many people with, "Has anyone told you how much they appreciate you today? Well, if not let me." Or, "Has anyone told you what a good job you're doing?" He is an encourager, an appreciator, and, in turn, a motivator.

An interesting difference between bees and buzzards is this: Bees are too busy doing what they are supposed to be doing to tear into others. Buzzards only eat off what others do. Ever see a buzzard do his own hunting? No, he survives off what others do. There are, unfortunately, examples of buzzards in the kingdom; but, to give an example of one here would be acting like a buzzard. You know your own examples.

John Powell made a statement in one of his books that may help you understand the buzzards. "Every obnoxious quality in another person is their cry of pain and plea for love!" Kids become discipline problems in order to get attention when love is lacking. Adults simply develop obnoxious adult behavior to get attention when what they really want and need is love. Don't let the buzzards get you down. They are in the bleachers and on the bench of every team. Just love them to death. And maybe the buzzard will die and a honeybee will be born!

Strategy Ideas

Jesus had an illustration not unlike the bees and the buzzards. It is the story about the log and the speck (Matthew 7:3-5). How much easier to see the log in another's eye! If you see logs in others' eyes, be careful. Jesus said the log is really in yours. The following chart is a work sheet to help you grow. It is a mirror on paper. Give it a try. Pick an individual like your mate, child, parent, or boss. Make a list of some of their major faults. (Yes, you get to play buzzard!) Now make a list of all of your poor responses or reactions to each fault. That is, start identifying some areas in which you need to grow in your life. Do it quickly; that will take the attention off the others and onto you. (Buzzard game is over.) Then make a list of how you can positively change your responses to each of their faults. You will be a much happier, sweeter person!

List six faults of one person,	List at least six of your poor reactions to each of their faults.	List how you can change your response to these characteristics.
EXAMPLE: Wife—she doesn't pay enough attention to me.	1. Withdraw. 2. Try to get even. 3. Talk about her (gossip). 4. Don't forgive her. 5. Put my energy in other things. 6. Belittle her. 7. Nag.	1. I'm going to pay attention to her anyway. 2. Dress nicely for her. 3. Smile at her. 4. Talk nicely to her. 5. Express my love for her. 6. Be physically affectionate. 7. Be verbally praising and polite.
1.		
2.		
3.		
4.		
5.		
6.		

Personal Planning

T R A I N

"All Scripture is God-breathed and is useful for teaching, rebuking, correcting and training in righteousness, so that the man of God may be thoroughly equipped for every good work."

—2 Timothy 3:16

Daily Training Verses

1. Ephesians 4:29
2. James 3:9-12
3. James 4:11, 12
4. Luke 6:37, 38
5. Proverbs 10:14, 31, 32
6. Matthew 7:3-5

T—TEACH. What does this passage teach me?	R—REBUKE. Does the passage correct me in any way? Am I satisfied with the extent to which I am applying it?	A—APPLY. If I applied this passage to my life, would I start or stop anything? What? Visualize it.	I—INITIATE. If I can start or stop something, when will I do it? Today? How? With whom?	N—NEEDS. I need to pray. (Follow the ACTS pattern: Adore, Confess, Thank, Supplicate.)
T	**R**	**A**	**I**	**N**

KNOWING YOUR POSITION ON THE TEAM

The church is the representation/extension of Christ in the world. When Jesus confronted Saul of Tarsus for persecuting the church, Jesus asked Saul, "Why do you persecute me?" The church is "the body of Christ" (1 Corinthians 12:27). The body of Christ is here to carry on what Christ would do if He were here himself—reconcile men to God (2 Corinthians 5:18-20).

In order to get that task done, we must function as a whole, healthy body. Any less means we won't reach God's goal as effectively and fully as desired by God. All Christians are part of the body. Each of us has a specific God-given role, task, or function. The God who designed our bodies, with all of their various dependent, inter-acting parts, yet differing functions, is the same God who designed the church body. If a physical body doesn't cooperate with the will of the mind, if certain functioning parts of the body do not work, we say it is handicapped or crippled. In both cases, the body may still function and even excel in some areas, but it likely will not reach the potential it could have if it were whole.

In 1 Peter 2:4, 5, Peter says we are spiritual stones being built into a spiritual house. In building a house, there is an entire army of people involved in the various stages. For example: financiers, developers, city planners, inspectors, architects, surveyors, graders, road crews, electricians, cabinet makers, appliance crews, air conditioning/heating workers, landscapers, carpet crews, cleaning crews, interior decorators, and real estate people. How many of these people would you like left out of the construction of your house? Not many! The quality, efficiency, and looks of the house would seriously be affected if workers started saying, "Oh, I'm just a plumber; I'm not important; they don't need me!" "Nobody will miss me; I'm just an electrician; they can get along without me." "I've got more important things to do than build the frame for that house!"

In order to get the spiritual house built, all the stones must be in place. If they aren't, there will be holes all over the house! God doesn't want or deserve a shabby house! Let's not let our neighbors in the community draw bad conclusions about the owner of the house (God) because the house looks unkept and unfinished because some aren't doing their jobs.

We all need to discover our gifts or ministries for Christ and use them. We can try different ministries, seek the opinions of other Christians about ourselves, train and develop ourselves for Christ. *What we are is God's gift to us, and what we become is our gift to God.* Our gift has been given to us because it is needed in the body! Each is to appraise his own talent intelligently and use it. Are you a functioning part of the body, or are you spastic, "doing your own thing," or are you a cripple? As one preacher said, "Either you have a gift, or God is a liar!"

Strategy Ideas

List any talent, skill, ability, or gift you have that can be used for the body and help advance Christ's cause. Ask T.E.A.M. members for their ideas and insights.

How can you use these gifts to the greatest extent? In the "Use" column, list ideas for using your gifts. Then number them in order of their priority and importance to Christ and the church.

Gift	Priority	Use

Personal Planning

T R A I N

"All Scripture is God-breathed and is useful for teaching, rebuking, correcting and training in righteousness, so that the man of God may be thoroughly equipped for every good work."

—2 Timothy 3:16

Daily Training Verses

1. 1 Peter 4:10, 11
2. Mark 10:45
3. Colossians 3:17, 23, 24
4. Ephesians 4:11-16
5. Romans 12:3-8
6. 1 Corinthians 12:7, 11, 12, 13, 18, 24, 25, 27

T—TEACH. What does this passage teach me?

R—REBUKE. Does the passage correct me in any way? Am I satisfied with the extent to which I am applying it?

A—APPLY. If I applied this passage to my life, would I start or stop anything? What? Visualize it.

I—INITIATE. If I can start or stop something, when will I do it? Today? How? With whom?

N—NEEDS. I need to pray. (Follow the ACTS pattern: Adore, Confess, Thank, Supplicate.)

T	R	A	I	N

GETTING TO KNOW THE TEAM MEMBERS

Fellowship is to the Christian what a huddle is to a football team, what a weekly meeting is to the salesmen of a business, what a teacher's meeting is to a school staff, what a briefing session is to the soldiers of an army, and what mealtime is to a family. Fellowship should also be pictured as the team breaking the huddle for the play, the salesmen hitting the streets, the teachers going to their rooms to teach, the soldiers going to the fields for maneuvers, and the family going to clean the house or yard, or going to work and school.

Fellowship is often seen as eating donuts and drinking coffee. That's a bad idea! Fellowship happens when Christians are active in preparing for and carrying out their ministries to advance the cause of Christ. The purpose of fellowship is to help us advance the cause of Christ. Fellowship is advancing the cause of Christ *together*. It involves our praying together, teaching together, calling and witnessing together, and giving together. It includes caring for each other's needs (1 John 3:16-18), confessing to one another (James 5:16), and encouraging one another (Hebrews 10:24, 25).

If we want to be like Jesus, we must fellowship with Christians. We must work with them, serve with them, pray, worship, warn, rejoice, and cry with them.

The purpose of the church is not to provide us with an isolated social club, but an active service center where Christians can help care for one another's needs as they reach out to the lost of the world.

Strategy Ideas

1. Identify the people with whom you are having Christian fellowship; that is, you are serving with them to advance the cause of Christ.

PEOPLE	PLACE	MINISTRY

Do you encourage them? How?

Do you pray for them? How often?

Do you share with them? In what ways?

Do you have Christlike care for them? How?

Do you cooperate with your leaders?

How can you be more faithful to those with whom you are now serving?

2. Do you need to be serving in a ministry with others more than you are now? If so, how?

Personal Planning

T R A I N

"All Scripture is God-breathed and is useful for teaching, rebuking, correcting and training in righteousness, so that the man of God may be thoroughly equipped for every good work."

—2 Timothy 3:16

Daily Training Verses

1. Hebrews 10:24, 25
2. 1 Thessalonians 2:7-11
3. 1 John 3:14-19
4. Romans 13:8-10
5. Galatians 6:1-4
6. Romans 15:1-3

T—TEACH. What does this passage teach me?	R—REBUKE. Does the passage correct me in any way? Am I satisfied with the extent to which I am applying it?	A—APPLY. If I applied this passage to my life, would I start or stop anything? What? Visualize it.	I—INITIATE. If I can start or stop something, when will I do it? Today? How? With whom?	N—NEEDS. I need to pray. (Follow the ACTS pattern: Adore, Confess, Thank, Supplicate.)
T	**R**	**A**	**I**	**N**

GETTING THE MOST OUT OF DOUBLES

God never planned that marriage be the relationship that provides two people with all they need in life (2 Corinthians 9:8-10). No mate (no matter how attractive, charming, intelligent, or talented that mate is) can do what God can do for you (provide eternal life, forgiveness of sins, and the Holy Spirit). But God certainly did want marriage to be a meaningful, good—yes, even a great—relationship. He wanted it to be a human object lesson of our relationship with Him.

A marriage can grow into a rut, or it can be a growing romance. Every husband and wife contributes to making the marriage one or the other. Next to Christ, God wants your mate to be most important to you. If you are married, you need to ask: "Am I really making my marriage a high priority? Am I giving my best to my mate? Or am I sitting around complaining, whining, pouting that I'm not getting all I want from my mate; so I'll use that as an excuse not to give my best?"

At a wedding, two people promise to give their best to each other regardless of their feelings or their careers, during good times and bad times, regardless of each other's good or bad traits! God wants us to have good marriages. In order to have one, a person needs to be the best mate he can be. What should he be and do? Read God's Word; He'll tell us what to do to have a good marriage. A married person needs continually to ask whether he is doing what God wants him to do to make the marriage the best it can be. If married couples do their Godly best, they'll be surprised what their marriages will be like.

Charlie Shedd, a minister and family/marriage writer and speaker, has told about a man who came to his office and moaned about how unloving, unromantic, and cold his wife was. He even suspicioned she was frigid! Charlie's response to the man was something like, "Well, Fred, after twenty-five years of marriage, you have just gotten what you deserve." That wasn't exactly what the man wanted to hear, but it was true. What one's mate is like after twenty-five years is a picture, most often, of what he has been to his mate.

What will your marriage be like in five, ten, twenty, or thirty years? You are having a big influence on it right now. Even if you are single, your actions, attitudes, and morals now will have an impact on any future marriage you enter. Are you looking at what you can get from a marriage, or are you concentrating on giving? Are you more concerned with what your mate is or isn't, or with what you are or aren't? If you are immature and selfish, you will concentrate on the imperfections of your mate to justify yourself. If you are mature, you will focus on what you should be, regardless of what your mate is. You won't use your own good conduct and kindness as a reward system for your mate's nice actions or hold back kindness as a punishment.

Strategy Ideas

For Singles:

1. What are the strengths in your life that would contribute to a strong marriage if you married?
2. What about you would need to change the most to help make a marriage succeed?
3. If you were to marry, what would you do to see that your marriage would be healthy?

For Marrieds:

1. Ask forgiveness of your mate for your failing in any particular areas (that you are aware of).
2. Share the wedding vows sheet with your mate this week. Plan a special time to do this.
3. At least once a month, plan a special, fun date.
4. Plan a getaway with your mate for a yearly honeymoon. If a honeymoon was good once, why not again? (Don't take the kids on these getaways.)
5. Read 1 Corinthians 13:4-8. Using the form below, put your name in the blanks. Read it as if you were your mate, kids, parents, and friends. Would they say yes or no to each item in regards to you? What areas do you have to grow in your love toward your mate and others?

Write your name in each blank below.
Would each of the following agree (A) or disagree (D) with each statement?

	Self	Mate	Kids	Parents	Friends	Enemy
_________________ is patient.						
_________________ is kind.						
_________________ does not envy.						
_________________ does not boast.						
_________________ is not (selfishly) proud.						
_________________ is not rude.						
_________________ is not self-seeking.						
_________________ is not easily angered.						
_________________ keeps no record of wrong.						
_________________ (done to him or her)						
_________________ does not delight when evil happens to others.						
_________________ always protects.						
_________________ always trusts.						
_________________ always hopes.						
_________________ always perseveres (hangs in there with).						
_________________ never fails.						

Personal Planning

Wedding Vows Sheet
(for use by married couples

Fill your names in the vows and look at each other with some meaning as you repeat and renew your vows. (It might be something to share with your kids too; they might get something special from it.)

Husband: I _____________________, take thee _____________________,
to be my wedded wife, to have and to hold from this day forward; for better, for worse; for richer, for poorer; in sickness and in health; to love and to cherish; til death do us part, according to God's holy ordinance; and, thereto, I pledge you my love.

Wife: I _____________________, take thee _____________________,
to be my wedded husband, to have and to hold from this day forward for better, for worse; for richer, for poorer; in sickness and in health; to love and to cherish; til death do us part, according to God's holy ordinance; and, thereto, I pledge you my love.

For a deeper time (if you think you can do it without getting defensive and turning it into an attack time), recall some of the following times in your life together in light of your vows.

To have and to hold	Are you holding each other enough?	Could you improve this some way?
For better	What have been some of your better times?	What could you do to have more
For worse	What have been some of your worst times? Don't attack, just share. Don't resurrect a dead issue.	What can you do to avoid worse times?
In sickness	Has the sickness of one or the other of you ever cause the other extra responsibilities? How have you handled it?	What could be done to make sick times more pleasant?
In health	Do you take your health for granted? How can you appreciate each other's health more?	Are there things you could be doing to help each other have better health?
To love and to cherish.	What does your mate do to love and cherish you?	What could you do to show your love and affection more?

Share with each other the things you are grateful for in your life together and the things you appreciate about the other.

T R A I N

"All Scripture is God-breathed and is useful for teaching, rebuking, correcting and training in righteousness, so that the man of God may be thoroughly equipped for every good work."

—2 Timothy 3:16

Daily Training Verses

1. 1 Corinthians 13:4-8a
2. Ephesians 5:21-33
3. Colossians 3:12-14
4. Proverbs 5:15-21
5. 1 Corinthians 7:1-4
6. 1 Peter 3:8, 9

T—TEACH.	R—REBUKE.	A—APPLY.	I—INITIATE.	N—NEEDS.
What does this passage teach me?	Does the passage correct me in any way? Am I satisfied with the extent to which I am applying it?	If I applied this passage to my life, would I start or stop anything? What? Visualize it.	If I can start or stop something, when will I do it? Today? How? With whom?	I need to pray. (Follow the ACTS pattern: Adore, Confess, Thank, Supplicate.)

T	R	A	I	N

NOT ON THE SCHEDULE

It's too bad that something as good as sex is enjoyed by so few. In fact, sex probably brings more anguish than it brings happiness. That's not the way it's supposed to be. Sex is supposed to bring physical, emotional, and spiritual fulfillment. In a day when sex is pursued by so many, who think it will bring them ultimate fulfillment in life from its physical dimension alone, it is really enjoyed by very few.

The problem is one of breaking the schedule determined by the Coach. Sex in its proper use, by God's schedule, is fulfilling. But the abuse of sex brings heartache and emptiness. Our culture (like many throughout history) is trying to squeeze all it can out of the physical dimension of sex, but it just can't find what it's looking for. The pursuit is like that of a water-starved man in the desert who finds a canteen with only a few drops of water in it. He desperately shakes it empty, to the very last drop, but he is not satisfied. In fact, his craving for water has increased. Pursuing the physical dimension of sex alone is equally unfulfilling.

Still, many are engaged in that pursuit. From the looks of our movies, cable and network TV, books, and magazines, sex seems to have become our society's new indoor sport. Some people play the game the way they play racquetball: whenever, wherever, and with whomever they can! They search for the "thrill of victory"; but by pursuing sex outside the context God designed for it, they ultimately find only the "agony of defeat."

God really does intend for sex to be delightful and enjoyable—even fun. But He put it in the context of the safety and security of marriage. He designed it, as He designed us. He knows better than we what is best for us in this regard. We try to judge by our experience, but our experience is limited. Only God has the omniscience of the Creator. He can be trusted; His Word is reliable. And He says that sex is for married couples only.

Christians are not immune to sexual temptations and struggles. In fact, for them the struggle may be more intense. Guilt becomes part of the problem, whereas a non-Christian may feel no guilt because he has no moral values regarding sex.

As a Christian, you know that sex at its best is confined to one mate in a growing relationship of love and trust (marriage). Yet you need not feel guilty because you have normal human sexual drives, attractions, or even temptations. At the same time, you must not think you are harming yourself by disciplining those drives. Every athlete denies himself certain attractive things in order to perform and achieve at his best. He does so at the direction of his coach, whose judgment and experience he trusts. God, our great Coach, wants what is best for us. He has scheduled sex to occur only in marriage with one mate. That's what is best.

Sexual abuse is sin: against Christ, against oneself, and against the other person involved (1 Corinthians 6:13-20). Why? It robs everyone of the best! The answer to strength in sexual discipline is Christ and growing in Him. It is found in loving Him, your mate (or your future mate), and yourself enough that you will not damage the possibility of being the best later in order to have a fling now.

Misuse of sex and lack of self-discipline can ruin your ministry and effectiveness for Christ. Don't give in to it. If you already have, confess your failure and repent. God can, and will, forgive. He can restore you to a role of service for Him. He can heal your damaged relationships.

Don't tempt yourself. Be careful about what you read, watch, and listen to. Strengthen yourself by growing in Christ. Stick to His schedule.

Strategy Ideas

DEALING WITH SEX

What do you *watch* that may tempt, weaken, or compromise your becoming Christlike? (movies, TV shows, pictures, etc.)	What do you, or could you, *watch* to strengthen yourself in regards to a healthy Christlike view of sex?

What do you *listen to* that may tempt, weaken, or compromise your becoming Christlike? (music, stories, people, radio stations, etc.)	What do you, or could you, *listen to* in order to strengthen yourself in regards to a healthy Christlike view of sex?
What do you *read* that may tempt, weaken, or compromise your becoming Christlike? (magazines, novels, stories, etc.)	What do you, or could you, *read* to strengthen you in regards to a healthy Christlike view of sex?
What do you *do and/or dwell on* that may tempt, weaken, or compromise your becoming Christlike?	What do you, or could you, *do* to strengthen yourself in regards to a healthy Christlike view of sex?
Where do you *go* that may tempt, weaken, or compromise your becoming Christlike?	Where do you, or could you, *go* in order to strengthen yourself in regards to a healthy Christlike view of sex.

Personal Planning

T R A I N

"All Scripture is God-breathed and is useful for teaching, rebuking, correcting and training in righteousness, so that the man of God may be thoroughly equipped for every good work."

—2 Timothy 3:16

Daily Training Verses

1. Ephesians 5:3-7
2. Titus 2:11-15
3. 1 Thessalonians 4:3-8
4. 1 Corinthians 6:18-20
5. Philippians 4:8, 9
6. 1 John 5:3-5

T	R	A	I	N
T—TEACH. What does this passage teach me?	**R—REBUKE.** Does the passage correct me in any way? Am I satisfied with the extent to which I am applying it?	**A—APPLY.** If I applied this passage to my life, would I start or stop anything? What? Visualize it.	**I—INITIATE.** If I can start or stop something, when will I do it? Today? How? With whom?	**N—NEEDS.** I need to pray. (Follow the ACTS pattern: Adore, Confess, Thank, Supplicate.)

RUNNING THE FARM LEAGUE

In this wild twentieth-century world, a quality relationship between parent and child beyond the childhood years doesn't exist a great deal. Families fail to share meaningful dialogue and seldom express appreciation for each other. A family needs to provide the love, respect, and understanding that remains for the most part absent in the insensitive outside world. Family members can improve the quality of their relationships with the rest of their family by verbalizing their appreciation, striving to understand the others' feelings, and helping other family members to understand their feelings.

Parents need to develop the ability to see through their children's bad traits to appreciate their many good qualities and deeds. These qualities can be affirmed with a smile, a wink, a squeeze on the hand, a kiss, a note on a pillow, an arm across one's shoulder, or a big bear hug. Parents can imagine their child is someone else's for a moment. That fresh perspective should enable them to find many positive qualities. Kids can do the same for their parents. If family members treated each other with the courtesy they do outsiders, the atmosphere in most homes would really improve.

Dr. Alice Ginott recommends that parents speak a loving language that makes their kids feel wanted and appreciated. That kind of language is foreign to many of us. Family members need to work at trying to understand the others' positions in life and to understand their feelings. Parents can often forget what it was like to go through the childhood and teen years. Kids often give little or no thought about the task of being an adult and parent. A little understanding can go a long way. It wouldn't hurt family members to read books written for parents and/or for kids on understanding other family members and how to improve family life.

Parents and kids alike need to remember that parents aren't running for a popularity contest. There are times they have to make decisions that won't be popular with the kids. The kids will not like their decisions. But the parents still have to make those decisions, and both they and the kids have to live with those decisions. The parents cannot fail to discipline because their kids will react negatively.

Families need to plan to spend time together. They need to plan to do things that years later they will look back on with fond memories. Kids need to be allowed the freedom to do their own things and go their ways as the years roll along, but some good family times to experience together and look back on will enrich any life.

A successful family life is filled with difficult times. It takes a lot of understanding, gentleness, patience, and work. It demands a lot of forgiveness and overlooking the other's weaknesses in some areas. It takes a desire to treat the others with respect.

Strategy Ideas

For Parents—
1. Hug each member of your family every day this week. Tell them that you love and appreciate them. This may feel strange if you haven't been doing it, but do it anyway.
2. Make a date with each of your children this month; take them out to eat, to a movie, shopping, or something else, something special that they like to do. Do it monthly.
3. Read a book on family relationships/communication in the family.

Recommended Reading
1. *Preparing for Adolescence*, Dr. James Dobson
2. *Promises to Peter*, Charlie Shedd
3. *Good Times for Your Family*
4. *Getting Your Family Together*

For Kids—
1. Hug each member of your family, every day this week. Tell them that you
   appreciate them and love them.
2. Make a list of how you can be more appreciative, supportive, and courteous
   to your family. What could you do to show your love to them?

Personal Planning

T R A I N

"All Scripture is God-breathed and is useful for teaching, rebuking, correcting and training in righteousness, so that the man of God may be thoroughly equipped for every good work."

—2 Timothy 3:16

Daily Training Verses

1. Proverbs 22:6
2. Deuteronomy 6:4-9
3. Ephesians 6:1-4
4. Colossians 3:18-21
5. Proverbs 13:24; 19:18
6. Proverbs 23:13, 14; 29:17

T—TEACH. What does this passage teach me?	R—REBUKE. Does the passage correct me in any way? Am I satisfied with the extent to which I am applying it?	A—APPLY. If I applied this passage to my life, would I start or stop anything? What? Visualize it.	I—INITIATE. If I can start or stop something, when will I do it? Today? How? With whom?	N—NEEDS. I need to pray. (Follow the ACTS pattern: Adore, Confess, Thank, Supplicate.)
T	**R**	**A**	**I**	**N**

THE COACH WON'T ALWAYS BE THERE TO PUSH YOU!

Abraham Lincoln, Michelangelo, Leonardo da Vinci, Billy Graham, Louis Pasteur, Helen Keller, Ben Franklin, Winston Churchill, the apostle Paul, Johnny Unitas. These individuals, like most who succeed or achieve in sports, politics, science, business, or the arts, have a common trait. It is called self-discipline or self-control. One won't be successful at marriage, parenting, a career, athletics, or ministry without it. Many factors can keep us from being self-disciplined or self-controlled: laziness, abuse of luxury, too much TV, wrong goals, sinful desires, irresponsibility, feelings, and a number of others.

Everyone is self-controlled! It's simply a question of what we allow to control the self. That's entirely our choice. We can let selfish ends, laziness, comfort, wealth, popularity, pleasure, pride, power, or Christ control self. Living for the flesh is living for self only. Spell *flesh* backwards and eliminate the *h*.

We can't be like Jesus without self-control.

Self-control is bringing myself under the control and discipline of Jesus! The marines claim to build men. Football coaches claim football builds character. What they both build is discipline.

As one submits himself to the authority and direction of the sergeant or coach, he is helped to become what he needs to be and to get the job done. It's the same with Jesus! An undisciplined person can ruin a job, a marriage, a friendship, a Sunday-school class, or a church. Self-discipline is saying no to those things that would interfere with achieving God's will and saying yes to what will advance it.

A lack of self-discipline is watching TV when I should be praying, studying, visiting, or playing with my kids.

A lack of self-discipline is working when I need to be playing.

A lack of self-discipline is playing when I need to be working.

A lack of self-discipline is reading when I need to be talking.

A lack of self-discipline is talking when I need to be reading.

A lack of self-discipline is spending when I need to be giving or saving.

A lack of self-discipline is hoarding when I need to be spending.

Strategy Ideas

What am I failing in or underachieving in now because of lack of self-control/discipline? Be specific.

Yes	No		If yes, what can I do to be more disciplined?
		In my ministry?	
		In my work?	
		In my home?	
		In my health?	
		In my relationships?	

What might I do if I were more self-disciplined? Dream some dreams!
What might I do. . . ?

in souls won ____

in ministry ____

in missions ____

in what I give ____

in my marriage ____

in books read ____

in friendships built ____

in other useful achievements _______________________________________

in writing articles, books, poems, letters _______________________

in exercising ____

in new skills ____

in quality time with the kids _______________________________

REMEMBER—They didn't build Rome in one day! How about a little at a time.
What could you do with one half hour a day for five days a
week? In five years, this would equal more than 650 hours!

Personal Planning

T R A I N

"All Scripture is God-breathed and is useful for teaching, rebuking, correcting and training in righteousness, so that the man of God may be thoroughly equipped for every good work."

—2 Timothy 3:16

Daily Training Verses

1. 1 Peter 4:7
2. 2 Peter 1:6, 8, 9
3. Galatians 5:22, 23
4. Titus 2:11, 12
5. 1 Thessalonians 5:6
6. 2 Timothy 1:7

T	R	A	I	N
T—TEACH. What does this passage teach me?	R—REBUKE. Does the passage correct me in any way? Am I satisfied with the extent to which I am applying it?	A—APPLY. If I applied this passage to my life, would I start or stop anything? What? Visualize it.	I—INITIATE. If I can start or stop something, when will I do it? Today? How? With whom?	N—NEEDS. I need to pray. (Follow the ACTS pattern: Adore, Confess, Thank, Supplicate.)

PLAYING WITH PAIN!

Suffering is an aspect of life that all of us have to deal with. As Christians, we are not less susceptible to suffering than are those who are not in Christ (Matthew 5:45). It may be that at times, we suffer more in many different ways than we did before we became Christians. We are told by Scripture that we share at least in part with the sufferings of Christ because we are one with Him. But what sets us apart from others is the joy we have because we can be victors over suffering; and suffering can actually be used as a vehicle for spiritual growth and a deeper relationship with Christ. In essence, situations that potentially could destroy our lives can be turned into growing experiences. This is why Paul could say in Romans 8:37 that "we are more than conquerors through Him who loved us." Suffering will remain until mortality puts on immortality (1 Corinthians 15:51-54). God's ultimate glory will be ultimate victory over all sin and evil (Revelation 21:1-1).

Suffering is not always caused by sin or a lack of spirituality (Job 1:6—2:10; 1 Corinthians 4:9-14; John 9:1-3).

Suffering can be a warning system, an indicator or deterrant to continued bodily or emotional harm.

Suffering causes us to focus our hope on the future (1 Peter 1:6, 13).

Suffering allows us to comfort others who suffer (2 Corinthians 1:3-11).

Sufferings are temporary (Romans 8:18-21).

Suffering can be used by God to refine, perfect, strengthen, and help us from falling (Hebrews 2:10; 12:10; Romans 5:3, 4; James 1:2-4).

Suffering can be positive or negative depending on how you respond.

Suffering can be used by God to strengthen us, or by Satan to turn us aside (1 Peter 5:8-10).

Suffering teaches obedience and self-control (Hebrews 5:8).

Suffering voluntarily is a way to show love to God (2 Corinthians 8:1-9).

Strategy Ideas

List instances when you have gone through suffering or adversities in recent years. Then list your responses and the results of your responses. Finally, list how you could have responded with a more Christlike attitude. How would that have made a difference in your growth?

Occasion of Suffering	Response and Results	Better Response/Possible Results

Personal Planning

GOD LEADS A PRETTY SHELTERED LIFE!

At the end of time, billions of people were scattered on a great plain before God's throne. Some of the groups near the front talked heatedly, not with cringing shame, but with belligerence!

"How can God judge us? How can He know about suffering?" snapped a joking brunette. She jerked back a sleeve to reveal a tattooed number from a Nazi concentration camp. "We endured terror, beatings, torture, and death!"

In another group, a black man lowered his collar. "What about this?" he demanded, showing an ugly rope burn. "Lynched for no crime but being black! We have suffocated in slave ships, been wrenched from loved ones, and toiled till only death gave release!"

Across the plain were hundreds of such groups. Each had a complaint against God for the evil and suffering He had permitted in His world. How lucky God was to live in Heaven where all was sweetness and light, where there was no weeping, no fear, no hunger, and no hatred. Indeed, what did God know about what man had been forced to endure in this world? "After all, God leads a pretty sheltered life," they said.

So each group sent out a leader, chosen because he had suffered the most. There was a Jew, a black, an untouchable from India, an illegitimate person, a person from Hiroshima, and one from a Siberian slave camp. In the center of the plain, they consulted with each other. At last, they were ready to present their case. It was rather simple: before God would be qualified to be their judge, He must endure what they had endured. Their decision was that God "should be sentenced to live on earth—as a man!"

But, because He was God, they set certain safeguards to be sure He could not use His divine powers to help himself.

Let Him be born a Jew.

Let the legitimacy of His birth be doubted, so that none will know who is really His father.

Let Him champion a cause so just but so radical that it brings down upon Him the hate, condemnation, and eliminating efforts of every major traditional and established religious authority.

Let Him try to describe what no man has ever seen, tasted, heard, or smelled.

Let Him try to communicate God to men.

Let Him be betrayed by his dearest friends.

Let Him be indicted on false charges, tried before a prejudiced jury, and convicted by a cowardly judge.

Let Him see what it is to be terribly alone and completely abandoned by every living thing.

Let Him be tortured and let Him die! Let Him die the most humiliating death—with common thieves.

As each leader announced his portion of the sentence, loud murmurs of approval went up from the great throng of people. When the last had finished pronouncing sentence, there was a long silence. No one uttered another word. No one moved. For suddenly, all knew: God had already served His sentence!

"I COULDN'T CARE MORE!"
—Jesus

God is with us. That is no answer for suffering. It is an answer to the sufferer. God gives us no platitudes, no proverbs. He gives presence.

When Jesus spoke of suffering, He gave no easy answers. He told us simply that God is with us. He knows and notices the smallest things: a sparrow's death, a falling hair, a wilting lily.

Jesus gave no logical, philosophical explanation of how tragedies may strike or why. He only assured us that it was not His Father's will that anyone, not even the littlest of us, should perish.

Jesus gave no theological justification for all the evil and pain that surround us.

He gave us Himself, the clearest demonstration of how far God's suffering love will go.

by David Augusburger
Moody Press

T R A I N

"All Scripture is God-breathed and is useful for teaching, rebuking, correcting and training in righteousness, so that the man of God may be thoroughly equipped for every good work."

—2 Timothy 3:16

Daily Training Verses

1. Romans 5:3, 4
2. James 1:2-8
3. 1 Peter 1:6, 7; 5:10, 11
4. 2 Corinthians 12:9, 10
5. Romans 8:18-21, 35-39
6. Hebrews 12:3, 4, 7

T—TEACH. What does this passage teach me?	R—REBUKE. Does the passage correct me in any way? Am I satisfied with the extent to which I am applying it?	A—APPLY. If I applied this passage to my life, would I start or stop anything? What? Visualize it.	I—INITIATE. If I can start or stop something, when will I do it? Today? How? With whom?	N—NEEDS. I need to pray. (Follow the ACTS pattern: Adore, Confess, Thank, Supplicate.)

T	R	A	I	N

KNOWING THE OPPOSITION

As we strive to live our lives committed to the purpose of advancing the cause of Christ in our own personal lives and throughout the world, it is important to realize our efforts are being opposed at every possible point by Satan. As Paul tells us in Ephesians, we are not struggling against mere human beings, but against spiritual forces. In order to fulfill our purpose as Christians, we need to recognize who our adversary is in this struggle. We need to learn what we can about the opponent from our scouting report (the Bible).

Satan was first one of the most important beings in Heaven, but he was cast out because of sin (Luke 10:18). Even though Satan has been defeated through Christ (Colossians 2:15), he has been trying to shipwreck the plan and purpose of God by seeking to cause man to reject God (2 Corinthians 4:4), or to stumble, or to compromise in his life with Christ. Satan's desire is to be like the most high; he wants to be God! His program is to keep men as his subjects, to satisfy them so they won't desire to be in God's kingdom.

The word *devil* means slanderer. The devil's plan of attack is to slander God to man (Genesis 3:1-7:). He also seeks to slander man to God (Job 1:9-12; 2:1-7). Man has the choice in his life of being the servant of one of two kingdoms, God's or Satan's (Acts 26:17, 18; Colossians 1:13).

The need for the Christian is to deal with the problem of how to withstand the opposition successfully.

Paul, in speaking to the Ephesians, outlines the armor of God that the Christian needs to wear to withstand the attacks of the devil successfully.

> Put on the full armor, not just part of it.
> Wear the belt of *truth*. Truth is the Word.
> Wear the breastplate of righteousness. Jesus is our righteousness.
> Have your feet fitted with readiness that comes from the *gospel*.
> Take the shield of faith and the helmet of salvation,
> Wield the sword of the Spirit. The *Word* of God is the sword.
> "Pray in the spirit on all occasions with all kinds of prayers and requests. . . . Be alert, and always keep on praying for all the saints" (Ephesians 6:11-18).

Jesus defeated the devil with Scripture! In their well-known encounter in Matthew 4, Jesus answered Satan's every temptation with, "It is written" (vs. 4, 7, 10). Jesus didn't have any magical response. He knew the Scriptures. They were His sword to defeat Satan. Maybe the reason we are not more victorious in our defeating temptation is that we don't know the Word well enough.

Finally, we need to realize the fact that not only has Satan been defeated, but in the final Judgment, he will be banished from God's presence eternally (Revelation 20). Jesus is the victor!

Strategy Ideas
SATAN MATCH

Personal Planning

Draw a line from the passage to the title.

Matthew 13:39	1. The evil one
1 Peter 5:8	2. Your enemy the devil, a roaring lion
Revelation 12:10	3. The tempter
Matthew 13:19	4. The enemy, the devil
John 8:44	5. Great dragon, ancient serpent
1 Thessalonians 3:5	6. The accuser of our brothers
Revelation 12:9	7. Liar; father of lies
John 12:31	8. Prince of this world
2 Corinthians 4:4	9. The god of this age
Ephesians 2:2	10. Ruler of the kingdom of the air
Ephesians 6:11, 12	11. Angels who abandoned their home
Matthew 25:41	12. Rulers, authorities, powers of dark world
Jude 6	13. The devil and his angels

T R A I N

"All Scripture is God-breathed and is useful for teaching, rebuking, correcting and training in righteousness, so that the man of God may be thoroughly equipped for every good work."

—2 Timothy 3:16

Daily Training Verses

1. 1 John 4:4
2. Isaiah 14:12-15
3. 2 Corinthians 11:13, 14
4. 1 John 3:8
5. 1 Peter 5:8, 9
6. 2 Corinthians 2:11

T—TEACH. What does this passage teach me?	R—REBUKE. Does the passage correct me in any way? Am I satisfied with the extent to which I am applying it?	A—APPLY. If I applied this passage to my life, would I start or stop anything? What? Visualize it.	I—INITIATE. If I can start or stop something, when will I do it? Today? How? With whom?	N—NEEDS. I need to pray. (Follow the ACTS pattern: Adore, Confess, Thank, Supplicate.)
T	**R**	**A**	**I**	**N**